Happy
Halloween
This book belongs to:
____

COPYRIGHT 2017 BY FLORABELLA

TIPS AND TRICKS FOR USING THIS BOOK:

1. THESE DELIGHTFUL IMAGES HAVE BEEN CONVENIENTLY PLACED ON ONE SIDE OF THE PAGE TO PREVENT BLEEDING.

2. USE MARKERS, GEL PENS, COLORED PENCILS, OR CRAYONS. IF YOU PRESS DOWN HARD, YOU MAY WANT TO PLACE A SHEET OF PAPER BEHIND THE PAGE.

3. LIGHT SOME CANDLES AND CHOOSE YOUR FAVORITE AUTUMN DRINK, SO YOU CAN RELAX, REFLECT, AND REJUVENATE AS YOU COLOR THESE INSPIRATIONAL FALL IMAGES.

4. CREATE THE PERFECT HALLOWEEN SETTING WITH THESE HALLOWEEN IMAGES, FUN FACTS, FOLKLORE, QUOTES, AND POEMS.

5. REMEMBER, IT'S A BUNCH OF HOCUS POCUS NOT TO BELIEVE YOU CAN CREATE ANYTHING YOU IMAGINE!

ALL THE GREAT STORIES HAVE WITCHES IN THEM!

COPYRIGHT 2017 BY
FLORABELLA

WHY DO WE CELEBRATE HALLOWEEN BY WEARING COSTUMES?
AS FUN AND LIGHTHEARTED AS HALLOWEEN IS TODAY,
IT'S A COMBINATION OF HISTORY, RITUAL, AND RELIGION.

Day Of Dead

IRISH IMMIGRANTS INTRODUCED THE CUSTOM OF DRESSING IN MASKS AND COSTUMES IN THE 19TH CENTURY. THE TOWNSFOLK WANTED TO HAVE ONE NIGHT WITHOUT LAWS, SO THEY COULD DO ANYTHING THEY WANTED?

SO THE TOWNSFOLK DRESSED UP IN MASKS AND COSTUMES, ALLOWING THEM TO HIDE THEIR IDENTITIES IN THE COMMUNITY. THEY PLAYED MISCHIEVOUS TRICKS ON THOSE WHO DIDN'T GIVE THEM TREATS.

SPOOKY THINGS
ARE
GONNA HAPPEN!

ACCORDNG TO AN OLD IRISH PROVERB, "TO HAVE A RAVEN'S KNOWLEDGE" IS TO HAVE SUPERNATURAL POWERS. THE RAVEN IS ONE OF THE OLDEST AND WISEST OF ALL ANIMALS.

WHY DO WE BOB FOR APPLES ON HALLOWEEN?

ALTHOUGH MOST OF THE HALLOWEEN RITUALS DISAPPEARED IN BRITAIN DURING THE 16TH + 17TH CENTURY, GAMES SUCH AS APPLE BOBBING REMAINED PART OF THE FESTIVITIES. THE APPLE FLOATED IN A TUB AND WAS CAUGHT IN THE MOUTH. AFTER AN APPLE PEELING WAS RIPPED OFF, IT WAS THROWN OVER THE LEFT SHOULDER. THE SHAPE OF THE APPLE PEELING REVEALED THE INITIALS OF THEIR TRUE LOVE!
GOOD LUCK!

WHO IS MY
TRUE LOVE?

WHY DO WE CARVE PUMPKINS ON HALLOWEEN?

HERE'S ONE VERSION OF AN OLD IRISH STORY FROM EUROPEAN FOLKLORE AND A MAN NAMED "STINGY JACK." AFTER HE WAS REFUSED ENTRY INTO BOTH HEAVEN AND HELL, HE WAS FORCED TO ROAM THE EARTH WITH NOTHING BUT A PIECE OF CHARCOAL AS A LIGHT AND A HOLLOWED-OUT TURNIP CARVED INTO A LANTERN TO GUIDE HIS WAY IN THE DARK. ON HIS JOURNEY, HE SCARED CHILDREN AND ADULTS!

THE TOWNSFOLK FIRST CALLED HIM, "JACK OF THE LANTERN." THEN SHORTLY CHANGED HIS NAME TO "JACK O' LANTERN." AT FIRST, THE TOWNSFOLK CARVED THEIR LANTERNS OUT OF TURNIPS, POTATOES, AND BEETS. BUT FINALLY, THEY USED PUMPKINS, TO WARD OFF THE GHOSTLY SPIRITS.

TODAY, CARVING PUMPKINS IS AN ANNUAL FAMILY TRADITION. THIS OCTOBER, WHEN YOU'RE HOLDING A WARM GLASS OF CIDER AND A CARVING KNIFE, REMEMBER THE TALE OF "STINGY JACK." LIGHT SOME CANDLES, TURN OFF THE LIGHTS, AND SPOOK YOUR FAMILY WITH THIS GHOSTLY TALE!

Happy
Halloween

WHY IS THE DAY OF THE DEAD OFTEN CELEBRATED ON HALLOWEEN?

THE DAY OF THE DEAD CELEBRATION STARTS ON HALLOW'S EVE, OCTOBER 31ST, AND ENDS ON NOVEMBER 2.

ALTHOUGH THE DAY OF THE DEAD (DIA DE MUERTOS) IS A FESTIVAL TO CELEBRATE LOVED ONES WHO'VE PASSED, "DAY OF THE DEAD" COSTUMES AND TATTOOS HAVE BECOME INCREASINGLY POPULAR FOR HALLOWEEN.

WHY ARE THE COLORS ORANGE AND BLACK ASSOCIATED WITH HALLOWEEN?

THE COLOR ORANGE SYMBOLIZES AUTUMN HARVEST, WHILE BLACK SYMBOLIZES DEATH.

THE SCARIEST MONSTERS ARE THE ONES THAT LURK WITHIN OUR SOULS.
EDGAR ALLEN POE

I WILL ALWAYS LOVE YOU... TO THE TOMB AND BACK!

HAPPY
HALLOWEEN

ONLY A VAMPIRE CAN LOVE YOU FOREVER!

ONLY A VAMPIRE CAN LOVE YOU FOREVER!

THE ONLY THING WE HAVE TO FEAR IS FEAR ITSELF...
AND SPIDERS...

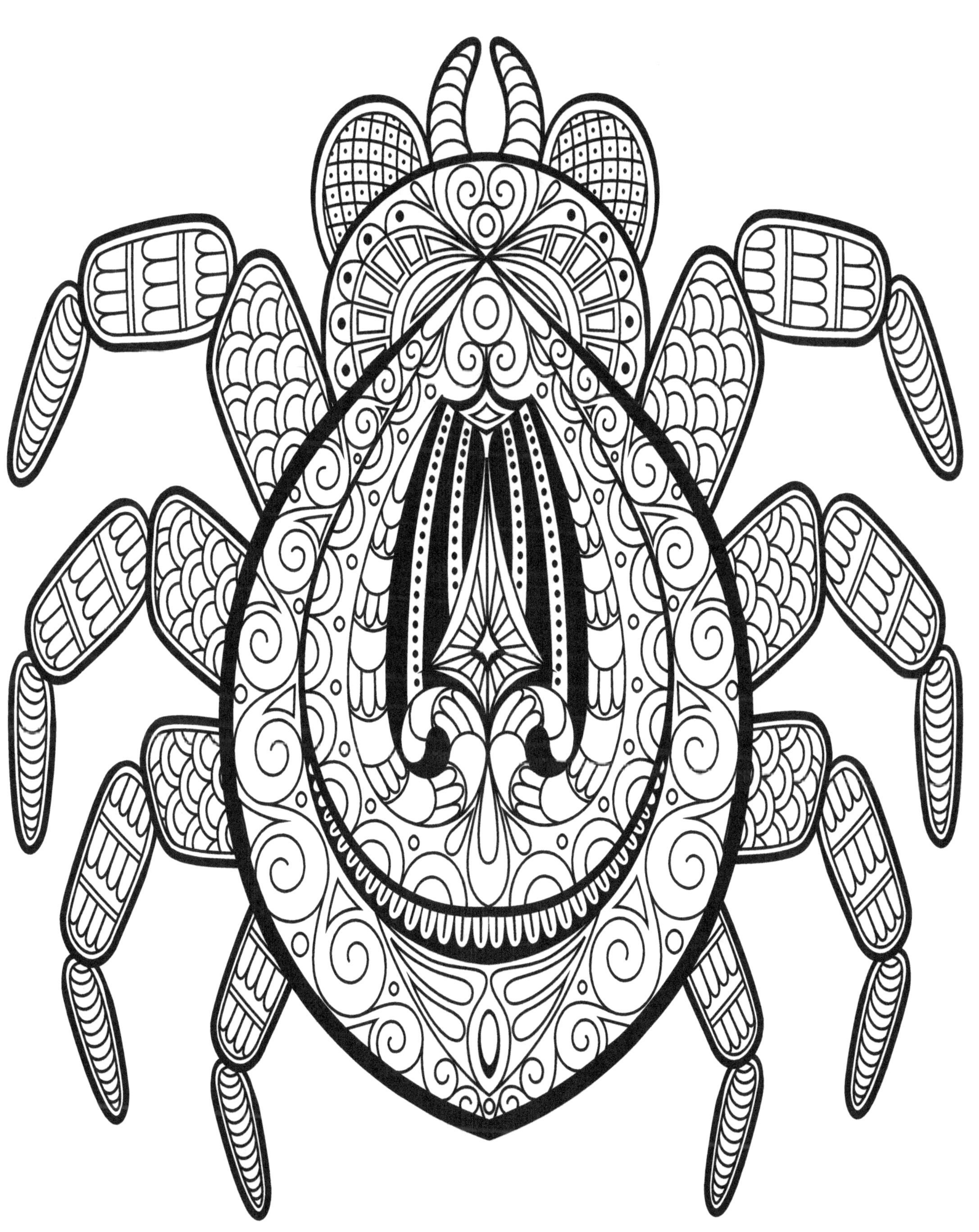

ON HALLOWEEN WITCHES COME TRUE,
WILD GHOSTS ESCAPE FROM OUR DREAMS,
EACH MONSTER DANCES IN THE PARKS.
HAPPY HALLOWEEN
NICHOLAS GORDON

Halloween Party
R.I.P.
JOIN US IF YOU DARE!
October 31st

THE LITTLE BAT
SCREAMED OUT IN FRIGHT
TURN ON THE DARK
I'M AFRAID OF THE LIGHT!
SILVERSTEIN

SHADOWS OF A THOUSAND YEARS
RISE AGAIN UNSEEN,
VOICES WHISPER IN THE TREES,
TONIGHT IS HALLOWEEN!
DANIEL KOZEN

I LOVE HALLOWEEN AND LOVE THAT FEELING:
THE COLD AIR, THE SPOOKY DANGERS
LURKING AROUND THE CORNERS.
EVAN PETERS

I LOVE HALLOWEEN AND LOVE THAT FEELING:
THE COLD AIR, THE SPOOKY DANGERS
LURKING AROUND THE CORNERS.
EVAN PETERS

COME WITH US AND YOU WILL SEE
THIS OUR TOWN OF HALLOWEEN!

COME WITH US AND YOU WILL SEE
THIS OUR TOWN OF HALLOWEEN!

I WISH I COULD WRITE AS MYSTERIOUS AS A CAT...
EDGAR ALLAN POE

WHEN WITCHES GO RIDING, AND BLACK CATS ARE SEEN,
THE MOON LAUGHS AND WHISPERS 'TIS NEAR HALLOWEEN.

MAGIC

NATURE IS A HAUNTED HOUSE~BUT ART~
A HOUSE THAT TRIES TO BE HAUNTED.
EMILY DICKENSON

EVERYDAY IS HALLOWEEN, ISN'T IT?
FOR SOME OF US...
TIM BURTON

SING A SONG OF HALLOWEEN PUMPKINS EVERYWHERE,
CATS AND BATS AND WITCHES ARE FLYING THROUGH THE AIR!

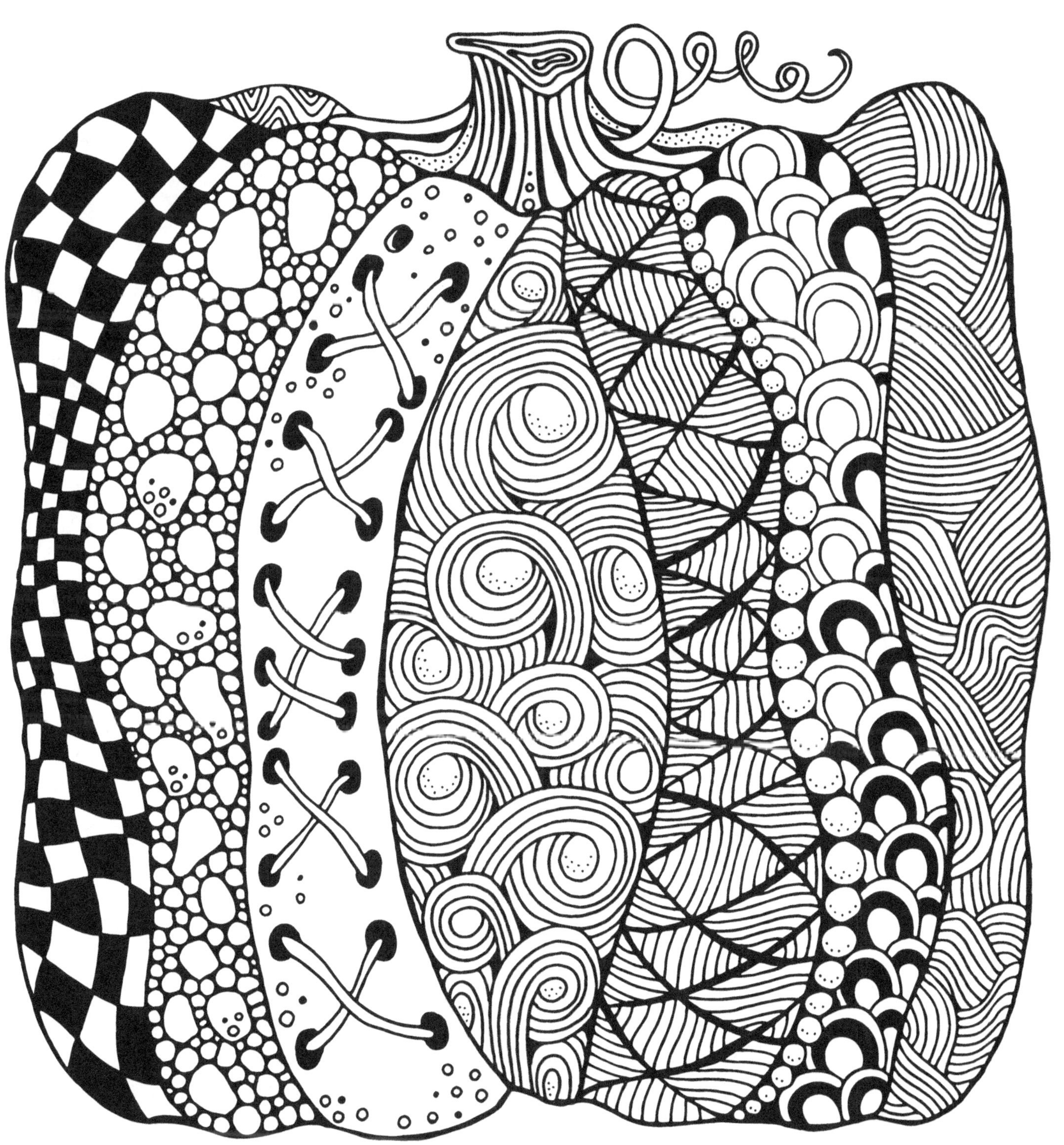

THERE IS NO BEAUTY WITHOUT SOME STRANGENESS.
EDGAR ALLAN POE

DEATH IS NOT THE GREATEST LOSS IN LIFE.
THE GREATEST LOSS IS WHAT LIES INSIDE US WHILE WE LIVE.
NORMAN COUSINS

DEATH IS NOT THE GREATEST LOSS IN LIFE.
THE GREATEST LOSS IS WHAT LIES INSIDE US WHILE WE LIVE.
NORMAN COUSINS

THINK
BELIEVE
DREAM
DARE!
R.I.P.

WHEN ALL IS LOST AND LOVE IS TRAGIC
CAST A SPELL
IT'S CALLED BLACK MAGIC!

GHOSTS AND GOBLINS
SPOOKS GALORE
SCARY WITCHES
AT YOUR DOOR
JACK 'O LANTERNS
SHINING BRIGHT
WISHING YOU A HAUNTING NIGHT!

IF YOU CAN'T STIR WITH THE BIG GIRLS,
STAY AWAY FROM THE CAULDRON.

WITCHES BREW

DO WHAT YOU FEAR
AND YOUR FEAR
DISAPPEARS!

DEEP IN THE EARTH MY LOVE IS LYING AND I MUST WEEP ALONE.
EDGAR ALLAN POE

RIP

STICKY FINGERS
TIRED FEET;
ONE LAST HOUSE,
TRICK OR TREAT!
RUSTY FISHER

AUTUMN:
PUMPKINS
FALLING LEAVES
HOT CIDER + TEA
APPLE PICKING
CRISP NOTHINGS
CHILLY NIGHTS!

Thank you for your recent purchase. We hope you're enjoying these delightful
coloring images, fun facts, quotes, folktale, and poems. Please visit our website for news about future books
and suggested friendly reads for children and adults by carefully
selected authors. Also, if there's a topic or subject you'd like us to write about, let us know.

YOU KNOW THE SAYING...
IF THE SHOE FITS...
GET A BROOM AND
A HAT TO MATCH!

florabellapublishing.com
florabellapublishing@yahoo.com
Florabella Publishing, LLC

A LITTLE WISH TO YOU FROM ME...
HAPPY HALLOWEEN!